EDUCATIONAL DEVELOPMENT PROGRAMS

Perceptual Training

by A. E. Tansley

**Communication
Skill Builders** ®
3130 N. Dodge Blvd. / P.O. Box 42050
Tucson, Arizona 85733
(602) 323-7500

About the Author

A. E. Tansley, B.Sc., M.Ed., is a well-known and respected expert in the field of early childhood development and remedial education in England.

His many years of experience and practical research as a teacher and as a staff inspector have formed the basis of both theoretical books for teachers and highly successful series for children, such as *Racing to Read* and *Sound Sense.*

The *Educational Development Programs* also stem from Tansley's wide experience of the education of young children, in particular from his work with teachers on in-service training courses.

Motor Education and *Perceptual Training* suggest ways in which these two aspects of early learning can be structured and integrated, so as to hasten children's acquisition of the basic skills essential to reading, writing, and number work.

American version published 1986, under license, by

Communication Skill Builders, Inc.
3130 N. Dodge Blvd./P.O. Box 42050
Tucson, Arizona 85733
(602) 323-7500

ISBN 0-88450-976-1   Catalog No. 7339

10 9 8 7 6 5 4 3 2 1
Printed in the United States of America

Contents

Foreword

These educational programs have resulted from in-service training courses designed to help teachers working with four- to nine-year-old children, and older children with learning and particularly reading problems. *Motor Education* (Tansley 1986) gives details of approaches to motor education and indicates the importance of children having good body awareness and appreciation of motor patterns and spatial relationships. The role of language as a mediator and controller of motor development is emphasized.

This program for the development of visual and auditory perception was originally devised as an attempt to improve the teaching of children with acute learning disabilities and difficulties. During the past twenty years or so, it has been modified and improved to help teachers of all young children. It has been extensively used in primary schools.

In using the suggestions given for perceptual training, teachers should bear in mind the absolute necessity of viewing them not in isolation, but as being closely related to and dependent upon other developmental areas: motor, language, thinking, emotional, and social. Research findings on the effectiveness of perceptual training have, admittedly, been equivocal. However, I believe that perception is a learned skill and therefore teachable.

The rather disappointing research findings are probably due partly to the research designs used, but perhaps more significantly to the fact that the training was specific and didactic. By this I mean that other related and contributory programs (for example, motor) were not used simultaneously, and above all, the role of language and giving the children verbal strategies to overcome their perceptual problems were largely ignored. Furthermore, some perceptual training programs have concentrated too much on nonverbal forms (such as geometric shapes) and neglected areas more directly related to reading.

Visual discrimination training as a preparation for early reading must involve work using association of letter forms, words, and maybe phrases, even though the children cannot name the letters or read the words. Again, in auditory perception training, discrimination must be extended to letters and words, and phonetic sounds and syllables in words, or words in sentences. My own experience in teaching strongly suggests that more intensive training in order and sequence, and in short-term memory for visual, auditory, and kinesthetic material is of great significance in preparation for basic work.

I hope that teachers will find the suggestions useful, use them with flexibility, and appreciate that the recommended programming of the activities is not applicable to all young children and learning failures—for some it will be too slow, for others further activities and consolidation may be essential. One further point must be stressed: teachers will rightly view this program as an ingredient in a learning readiness program. However, it is not necessary for the individual programs to have been completed before children are capable of making a satisfactory start in reading, writing, and early mathematics. Indeed, the principal aim is to hasten readiness for basic subjects.

A. E. Tansley
Birmingham 1980

Perceptual Training

The first comprehensive program for perceptual training was specifically related to the development of those skills which appeared to be involved in the visual and auditory decoding processes associated with early reading (visual discrimination, copying, memory, rhythm, sequencing, form perception, completion and closure, temporal sequencing, and auditory discrimination, memory, sequencing, and rhythm). The training was rather rigid and specific at first, although involving all the skills mentioned. With experience, and an increasing awareness of the role of language in training, the use of the program took on a wider meaning and became more dynamically associated with learning activities such as classification, motor activities (see Tansley 1986, *Motor Education*) seriation (in early number work), memory training, language development, music, and drama.

It was used initially in one-to-one teaching situations, but with a realization of its general application to all young children, the programming and organization of the materials were modified for group activities. Much of the work, particularly in visual perception, can be done with a minimum of equipment and materials using an overhead projector and worksheets. One further observation was that children could be held back in the acquisition of the perceptual skills by an overinsistence on use of paper-and-pencil responses. Some children's perceptual skills were grossly underestimated when they were assessed on a paper-and-pencil task. For example, in an activity such as drawing a triangle, it is wrong to assume that a child's inability to draw triangles means that the child has poor perception of triangles. The drawing of a triangle is a perceptual-motor task and not one of form perception, *per se.* The fact that a child cannot draw the triangle indicates a need for fine motor and hand-eye coordination work, or that the child has a specific learning disability in transducing visual information to a motor response, indicating the need for a program of training in kinesthetic-motor association.

This early work led to a greater understanding of the processes involved in perception, which can be defined as the process by which one interprets and makes use of information received through the senses. Visual perception comprises more than the ability to see in relation to visual acuity, depth vision, binocular vision, ocular pursuit, and fixation. It is a neurophysiological process whereby the visual energy generated on the retina and transmitted to the midbrain and cortical association areas is translated into meaning and related to past experiences, becomes usable to generate motor or vocal responses, and can be stored for future use.

It is possible for a child to have perfectly normal sight but to be perceptually blind or handicapped. The process of perception is one of interpreting all the stimulation transmitted by the sensory organs (eyes, ears, taste, smell, touch, and movement) resulting in appropriate responses to the environment and experiences. It follows that any deficiency in sensory reception will cause disturbance in the totality of perception. A corollary of this would seem to be that the more sensory information which can be used in learning, the greater the area of the brain being stimulated, the more efficient the learning process will be. Hence the need for holistic, multisensory, language-mediated learning in young children.

SENSORY CHANNELS AND INTEGRATION

The young child becomes a perceiving being as a result of receiving rich and varied sensory stimulation while moving about in space. By virtue of this moving and stimulation, the majority of children arrive at school age with adequate sensory skills to benefit from normal infant or nursery approaches. There are some children who, because of lack of suitable play experience, or because of learning disability, need a program of structured sensory stimulation to clarify sensory experience which has been inadequate or to which responses have been abnormal. Experience suggests that all children will benefit from the programs of perceptual training because often sensory training will lead to accurate perception, and specifically gear these senses to basic work.

The brain receives sensory information through six channels or modalities: visual, auditory, kinesthetic, touch, olfactory (smell), and gustatory (taste). The first four are of the greatest importance in school learning situations and teachers should ensure that they are functioning normally. It is, however, not proposed to deal with the diagnosis of individual sensory channel defects, but to give some suggestions in relation to sensory training.

The Visual Channel

Because reading depends upon good left-to-right eye tracking and fine control of the eye, it is recommended that training in ocular control be given to most children. The overhead projector is a useful aid in this connection. The children, with heads kept or held still, follow a stimulus moving at varying speeds from left to right across the screen. Other eye movements (vertical, diagonal, circular, and following outlines of objects and geometrical forms) can be practiced in the same way. This training can be very tiring and should not last for more than two or three minutes. It can be supplemented by asking the child to point to a target and follow its movements, giving hand-eye coordination training using big arm movements. It is useful to encourage the use of language in this training, using words such as *right, left, up, down, across, around, long, short,* etc. This *ocular pursuit training,* coupled with finger and arm movement and speech, has been of considerable help to many children in hastening form perception, visual discrimination, and closure.

The overhead projector can also be used for *training eye fixation.* Five known objects are displayed and the children fixate on the one named for a count of up to ten.

Another way of doing this is to have five or six pictures or shapes mounted on a piece of wood so that they can be raised or lowered individually as required. The child, with head still, fixates on the one which is raised. This will also make the child use peripheral vision as well as central.

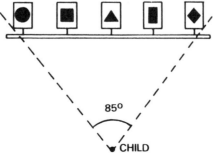

A variation on this can be used to draw the child's attention to detail. For example, with a picture of a house on the screen the child can be asked to look at the door, look at the window, look at the roof, look at the bedroom window on the right, etc.

It should again be emphasized that this training should not be carried on for too long at one session. This sort of material can also be used for training visual memory and sequencing.

THE TACTILE/KINESTHETIC CHANNELS

Tactile/kinesthetic channels are often neglected in preschool play activities. Touch sensitivity can be developed by getting children to feel different textures, without looking at them, and then grading them from rough to smooth, or hard to soft, etc. Using a "feely bag" to identify objects and shapes by touch is helpful and children should also learn to seriate by size, using only touch and to match pairs of objects, shapes, and textures by touch.

Kinesthesia (the internalized appreciation of movement) can be developed by exercises in which the child repeats body movements which the teacher has done by moving parts of the child's body when blindfolded (for example, raising the right arm, drawing a circle in the air with the right or left hand, stepping forward one pace and then one pace to the left). The kinesthetic sense is also involved in such activities as when the teacher draws a shape on the child's back and then the child draws the shape either in the air or using pencil and paper; or when the teacher, holding the child's hand, draws a shape or letter in the air and the child then draws the shape or letter, the child keeping eyes closed throughout.

Many of the body awareness, balance, and rhythm activities given in the motor education program are also useful in developing kines-thesia, since they include gross and fine muscle activity as well as movement appreciation. The four sensory channels, visual, auditory, kinaesthetic, and tactile are particularly important in learning. However, in most learning situations they are rarely involved singly. They usually function in various combinations and are almost always associated with some form of language and motor activity. In studying the learning development of handicapped children, the teacher comes up against the need for intensive work in sensory integration to develop compensatory activity to ameliorate the effects of an individual channel being closed or impaired. In past work with some very young children and the mentally handicapped, an intriguing problem was posed when they could see and hear well enough to learn and frequently had sufficient language for verbal strategies to have developed, yet they could not begin to read. The problem seemed to be one of difficulty in sensory channel integration or cross-modality function. It now seems that the development of perception, as defined above, is dependent not so much on sensory information being received through individual senses, but in cross-modality function mediated by speech and language. Perceptual training programs should include investigations into and programs for the growth of sensory channel integration. This will ensure that each child's sensory equipment will be understood. There are some children who at age five have strong visual and kinesthetic channels and a poor auditory channel. This has important implications for teaching, because such children are more likely to respond to a "look and say" method rather than a phonic approach in the beginning of reading. The reverse may also be indicated: a strong auditory channel and poor visual/kinesthetic channels indicate the need to use a phonic approach.

As a general rule, teaching should use the strong channel and train the weak one so that suitable combinations can be used. Certainly, good reading and spelling depend upon good visual/auditory/kinesthetic integration.

SUGGESTED ACTIVITIES FOR INVESTIGATING AND TRAINING CROSS-MODALITY FUNCTION

Visual/Auditory

1. Play or make a sound and ask the child to find the object or picture which goes with it.

2. Show an object, picture, word, letter, or numeral and ask the child to say when the appropriate sound is heard.

3. Activities similar to those above may be used to train memory (for example, remembering two sounds with eyes closed and the visual stimulus out of sight and then finding the objects).

Visual/Kinesthetic

1. Let the child copy a shape without being able to see hand movements. The overhead projector can be used for group activities. The teacher draws on the acetate sheet and children draw with hands out of sight, behind a board or curtain, as in the illustration on page 6.

2. The child, with eyes closed, holds a pencil while the teacher (or another child) guides the hand by holding the pencil and draws a shape, letter, or word in the air. The child now has to identify and select what was drawn from a visual display.

3. Repeat 2, but this time draw on the child's back.

Of course, the above activities have to be programmed to suit the child's age and ability. Experience suggests that a readiness for a "look and say" approach to reading, with regard to visual/kinesthetic integration, is indicated when the child can cope with a diamond shape, and maybe simple words.

The following programming is suggested. The length of time and speed of drawing on the child's back should also be varied, and it is important to introduce the appropriate language (for example, *long, short, middle, down, up, across, left, right, start, stop, quick, quickly, slow, slowly, fast*). The visual display can either be in view all the time or not produced until the drawing has been completed.

STIMULUS		VISUAL DISPLAY
1	|	| —
2	—	| —
3	+	| + —
4	L	L ⌐
5	⌈	L ⌐ ⌈
6	/	/ — |
7	\	/ \ L
8	×	| + ×

The program can then include simple shapes. For example, draw a diamond and ask the child to select from a display of a diamond plus three other shapes.

For some children, particularly those with difficulties in fine motor control, laterality (see Tansley 1986), visual discrimination, word-to-word matching, the above program should be extended to include letters, numerals, and words. For example, draw on a child's back the word "am." Ask the child to select the word from a card on which the words "on," "is," and "am" appear.

The visual/kinesthetic approach can also be used later to help children pay attention to fine differences in letters or words. For instance, a child may be confused over "green garden girl." With three words in view, start writing one on the child's back and ask the child to point to the correct word as soon as it is recognized. This can be repeated with the three words out of sight until the word has been written (that is, using kinesthetic memory more specifically). The integration can take place in the reverse direction. The child is shown a triangle and indicates when that shape or word is drawn on his back. This reversal of the process applies to all the integration functions mentioned.

Visual/Haptic

1. Without being able to see it, the child explores an object by feeling and then has to find the object by sight.
2. Repeat 1 using geometrical shapes and solid objects.
3. Repeat the above at a later stage for children who require it, using words, letter shapes, or words written by using sand on glue.
4. Repeat the above in reverse. For example, show a shape and ask the child to find it from two, three, or four shapes to be explored by feel.

Audio/Haptic

1. Ask the child to describe what is being explored and identify by feel; or to find a toy or shape described by the teacher or another child.
2. Blindfold the child. Make sounds and ask the child to find the object or toy which is making the sound. One way of doing this is to tape record animal sounds and ask the child to find the animal from a group of plastic models, or give the child an object, toy, or animal shape and ask the child to make or identify the sound which goes with it.

Visual/Motor

Only some of the more important modality functions have been mentioned. In exploring the environment, children use many combinations of functions in association with movement and language. There is much more to be discovered about these association and integration processes and the role language plays in them and their development. Nevertheless, the work described here is of great importance in hastening the development of perceptual skills, language, and the learning of basic subjects.

In all this work, the role of language and speech cannot be overemphasized. Teachers using the programs have frequently observed that they help in the development and organization of a language program. The role of language and speech in movement is stressed in *Motor Education* (Tansley 1986).

Useful Materials for Sensory Integration

Teacher-made:
    Feely bag
    Haptic board as in illustration
    Wire shapes
    Texture box and texture pairs
    Sand-on-glue cards of shapes and letters to feel
    Musical instruments
Teacher-made programs for sensory integration work

Commercially prepared:*
    Bean Bags (CP, Lake, DLM, Child)
    Tactile Dominoes (CP, Lake, Child)
    Feel by Touch (CP, Child)
    Pass the Bag, Feely Bag (Child)
    Multi-Texture Puzzles (CP)
    Feel and Match Textures (CP)
    Tactile Bridges (CP, DX)
    Multi-Shape Touch Board (CP)
    Listen, Look, Learn Audio-Visual ABC Kit (DX)
    Bag of 3-D Shapes (Lake)
    Look Hear (CS, Child)

---

*See page 57 for company names and addresses.

Training Visual Perception

The following elements in visual perception appear to be important in early learning: hand-eye coordination, form perception, visual discrimination, visual memory, sequencing and rhythm, closure, and completion. It is difficult to assess the relative importance of these in different areas of learning, and to determine the developmental levels necessary for successful achievement in decoding (as in early reading and number) and encoding (as in writing and spelling). The following programs are given as a guide to training the various skills and as a help in diagnosing the visual perception weaknesses which may be displayed by individual children.

The programs have necessarily to be given separately, but it is important to stress their interrelation and dependence on good motor and language development. Although hand-eye coordination may not seem to be a visual perception skill, it is dependent on kinesthetic perception and is an integral part of many visual perception and perceptual-motor activities. Visual perception results from an integration of all subskills. Its growth is facilitated by appropriate speech and language which will develop awareness of similarities and differences in color, size, shape and position, changes of position and orientation in space, and rhythmic and temporal sequencing. The result of using the individual programs in an integrated way, supported by language, should be to develop good visualization (including visual imagery) and classification skills based on generalized meanings, that is, conceptualization. The following example should illustrate the importance of integrating the programs.

Suppose the children have been working on different shapes of varying colors, sizes, materials and thicknesses, the teaching might include the following language and activities.

Classification
Show me a rectangle.
Are all the rectangles the same?
How are they different?
Yes, some are red, blue, or green.

How else are they different?
Yes, some are big and some are small.
Who has the smallest, largest, widest size?
How else are they different?
Yes, this is a thick one.
Who has a thin one, the thinnest one, the thickest one?
How else are they different?
Yes, this is a wooden rectangle and this is a plastic one.
Who has the thickest, biggest, blue wooden rectangle?
Susan, tell us about your rectangle. (Eventually, the reply should include all the attributes of Susan's rectangle.)

Position
1. The children have a large piece of white paper and an assortment of shapes. Using an overhead projector (or a piece of paper) the teacher places a shape in varying positions. The children place a shape in the same position, using the appropriate language to describe what they are doing.
2. The teacher moves a shape into varying positions and the children then move likewise, describing what they are doing.
3. The teacher changes the orientation (for example, with a rectangle, stands it on a line, under a line, above or below a line, on its longer or shorter side, at varying angles).
4. The teacher uses two rectangles and changes their relative positions. The children discuss and copy.
5. The teacher describes actions to be performed with the shape or shapes, and the children then respond by manipulating shape(s) accordingly.
6. The children make different rectangles.

Order
Using two or three shapes, the teacher shows sequences for the children to copy and then repeat from memory (see visual sequencing and visual rhythm programs).

Generalizing meaning
By discussion, the children arrive at a definition of the word rectangle. They are asked to find rectangular shapes in the environment: doors, windows, books, boxes, etc. They explore what happens when different or similar rectangles are put together to make similar or different patterns and objects. They make visually rhythmic patterns with rectangles of different sizes and colors, for example:

They create models with an assortment of rectangles.

It will be seen from the above teaching example that a tremendous amount of learning can be involved. The amount of oral language which can result should be noted. Indeed, it is a useful exercise to list the words which could be used in just this one teaching situation. The visual perception training involved includes training in color and shape recognition, form perception, visual memory and sequencing, hand-eye cordination, position in space, visual discrimination, and classification involving color, shape, size, and material.

TRAINING HAND-EYE COORDINATION

The training of hand-eye coordination and the development of fine motor control is referred to in *Motor Education* (Tansley 1986). Ocular pursuit activities are mentioned above. Many children arrive in school with these skills sufficiently well developed for them to be capable of copying shapes, drawing and painting simple pictures, and even beginning to write. It is important to realize that not all children will need to work through all or even any of these activities. As a guide, children who can hold a writing tool correctly, can draw firm, steady horizontal and vertical lines 8" long in one movement, or write names recognizably should not waste time on this program, but can go straight on to the writing program (see pages 16-17).

There is a sizeable group of four- and five-year-old children, and some older ones, who need specific training in hand-eye coordination as a preparation for handwriting. For perceptually handicapped children and those with neuromotor disturbance, the training is essential. For all these children, rich and varied play activities which emphasize hand-eye coordination will be helpful. Structured gross and fine motor activity (see Tansley 1986) must precede paper-and-pencil tasks. The following play and games activities are suggested.

1. Running cars and engines along tracks on the floor or painted on rolls of paper (for example, white tracks of varying widths and shapes on black paper)
2. Moving game pieces as in board games
3. Simple jigsaw puzzles and mosaics
4. Operation Game (Milton Bradley) where small parts must be carefully taken out or a buzzer will sound
5. Using construction toys (for example, Lego)
6. Lacing and sewing cards and threading beads
7. Tracing and drawing around large shapes

8. Using a magnet under a card to move a metal object along lines and around spaces and shapes marked on the card

9. Chalkboard activities, using big movements

10. Color shapes or stencils

11. Using scissors to cut along lines and around shapes

12. Paper-and-pencil work is introduced by the children, drawing along tracks which become progressively narrower, and finally joining dots (at increasing distances apart) to make lines, geometric shapes and outlines of animals, etc. The following programming is suggested.

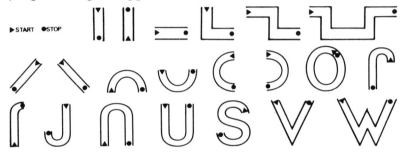

For most children, practice with only two widths appears to be necessary before drawing along lines or joining dots can be done satisfactorily.

13. The usual prewriting patterns should follow using a program based on the following suggestions.

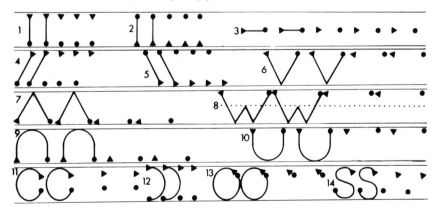

Some children may require an intermediate stage in which they join dots, for example:

14. Combinations of the patterns in suggestion 12 can also be used. Continuous movements should be encouraged where possible, for example:

Children with problems in fine motor skills and hand-eye coordination need intensive preparation at this prewriting stage. The following activities are suggested:

1. Further chalkboard work

2. Using prepared templates to feel and trace with the fingers, and later for drawing with crayons or pencils, for example:

3. Feeling plastic shapes or shapes painted in glue and then sanded over:

4. For all children, it is useful to encourage talking while tracing or drawing the lines and shapes, using the words *start, stop, straight, up, down, across, short, over, under, to the right, to the left, around, top, bottom.*

For example, down, to the right and stop.

Useful Materials for Training Eye-Hand Coordination*

Dubnoff School Program (DLM)
Dubnoff Write-On Cards (DLM)
Tracing Cards—Pictures and Patterns (DX)
Keep On Tracking Cards (CP, OL)
Eye-Hand Integration Exercises I, II (DLM)
See It, Do It (DLM)
Pegboards and design cards (DLM, Child)
Lacing games and activities (DLM, CP, Child, OL)
Hammer Board (OL)
Legos, Tinkertoys, other building systems (CP, Lake, Child)
Puzzles
Developmental Magnetic Mazes (Lake)

Teaching Handwriting

All the fine movements used in writing are covered in sections 12 and 13 of the activities for training hand-eye coordination. The suggested program for the teaching of handwriting has resulted from discussions with many teachers on in-service courses. It will not be acceptable to all teachers, since there are many styles of writing, but the program aims to reflect the preference of the majority. The important thing is that schools should have a program which—in the early stages at least—is systematically and consistently taught. The following points should be checked before the child begins to learn to write.

Sitting position

The child should have a chair and a desk or table of the correct height so that the feet are comfortably but firmly on the ground and the forearm rests on the desk top.

Handedness

The child's handedness should have been unequivocally established (see Tansley 1986, Cerebral Dominance) and good left-to-right tracking should have been acquired. Left-handed children require particular attention to avoid bad writing habits. The following suggestions should be helpful when teaching left-handed children.

---

*See page 57 for company names and addresses.

1. The writing movement of left-handed children, being toward the body, is more restricted than the away-from-the-body movements of the right-handed.

2. If chalkboard examples are used, the demonstration by a right-handed teacher may be confusing. The teacher's writing will follow the hand movement while the left-handed child's copying will precede the hand movement. This difference may be one cause of the proneness of left-handed people to reversals and mirror writing.

3. For left-handed children, the paper should be slightly to the left and tilted downward toward the child as in the illustration. The left elbow should be tucked into the side as the child writes with a pushing movement toward the body. The pen or pencil should point to the left shoulder. This will ensure that the child can see the writing, encourage left-to-right movement, and avoid smudging of the writing. It will also discourage the child from "hooking" the hand above the writing line in order to see the writing.

4. Left-handed children may require more encouragement and reassurance than right-handed children because they may feel different, particularly if any difficulty is over-emphasized.

5. The left-handed child should sit in such a position that the left arm does not interfere with a right-handed child's arm.

Grip

Children who have had plenty of experience in handling educational toys will usually grip the writing tool correctly from the start. In case of difficulty, a good way of demonstrating and practicing the correct grip is achieved by getting children to pick up marbles, pebbles, and small cubes. The thumb, index, and middle fingers will be used in the right positions. The pen or pencil should rest at the side of the middle finger and be guided by the slightly bent index finger for downward strokes and by the thumb for upward ones. The fourth and little finger should support the hand and rest gently on the paper. About two-thirds of the forearm should rest on the table, thus providing a firm base for the hand movement.

The nonwriting hand should rest on the paper or table and support the body. It might also be used to keep the paper immediately in front of the body midline.

Some children tend to hold the writing tool too firmly and to press too hard with the index finger. The grip should be such that the teacher can remove the tool from the child's hand by a gentle pull.

The above applies to both right- and left-handed children. However, for left-handed children, the grip should be slightly higher up the pen or pencil to allow a better view of the writing.

A Suggested Writing Program

It is suggested that the systematic teaching of handwriting should be introduced as early as possible, because writing is a great help in the acquisition of a sight vocabulary.

Using guidelines

There is much debate about the use of guidelines in the beginning stages of a handwriting program. Teachers must obviously relate this to children's needs, but children seem to benefit from their use, since they need help in determining and controlling the size and proportion of letters. The spaces between the lines is a matter of choice, but to begin with a space of one centimeter is suitable, later reduced to five millimeters. The base line should be thicker than the others, and some teachers prefer these to be broken.

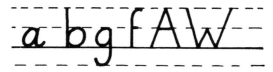

Children also need cues which indicate where to start and take off the pen or pencil. They may also require help in learning to get into the habit of using the correct movements and directions. (See below.)

What type of script should be used?

Printed script is almost universally used in the beginning stage of writing. In some respects this is a disadvantage since cursive script is more rhythmical and flowing and leads to joined script more easily and naturally. This program is a compromise between the two which seems to be acceptable to many teachers in primary schools. Capital letters are shown in the usual Roman style.

The grouping of letters

Different ways of grouping letters in initial handwriting teaching have been suggested. The reasons for grouping relate to considerations of ease of fine motor movement and the frequency of use in free writing. One further consideration of some significance is that letters occurring in the first words in a reading sight vocabulary should be taught early. This facilitates the writing of these words as an additional aid to their learning. Letters should be used to write words as part of the program, and these words can then be read, matched to words in books, used in oral work, and written by the children and used as flashcards. The following grouping attempts to reflect these considerations:

STICK FAMILY iltfjk   ROUND FAMILY ocadgq

rmnhbp   v   esuywxz

DOWN, UP AND OVER.   DOWN & UP   OTHERS

Practicing letter and word formations

1. Use guidelines one centimeter apart and start-stop cues, and encourage the children to speak as they trace or write over the individual letters, using one line of examples for each letter (for example, i—start, down, up, stop, dot; t—start, down, up, stop, start, across, stop, etc.). It is helpful to use a green dot for start and red for stop. All letters, except for *f, i, j, k, t,* and *x,* should be written with one continuous movement.

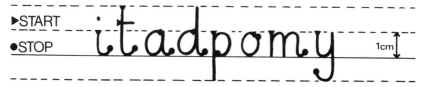

▶START
●STOP   itadpomy   1cm

2. Repeat the practice above with five millimeter spaces between the guidelines. For some children, intermediate stages may be needed between these in which dotted letters are given to be joined up. The distance between the dots can be widened if further practice is necessary.

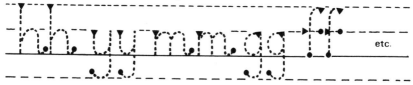

hh yy mm aa ff   etc.

3. Copying letters, first using guidelines and then freely.
4. Tracing, writing over, and free copying of words, preferably from the sight vocabulary being used by the child.
5. Some teachers may also prefer to teach the writing of numerals at this stage. However, if number teaching is based on the study of groups, it may be preferable to teach the numerals when the group, or set, for which they stand is being studied.
6. The final stage is, of course, teaching joined script. Since the hooks have been included in most letters in the above program, joining letters into words seems to follow naturally.

Useful Books and Materials*

The writing program can be made by teachers using duplicated sheets for all the stages. Writing programs for children with poor fine motor skills and hand-eye coordination problems should include the following activities.

1. Chalkboard work, using chalk
2. Feeling the shapes of plastic letters and papers made by sand sprinkled on glue or made of sandpaper or coarse material
3. Feeling letter templates cut out of cards
4. Feeling letters drawn in the sandtray by the teacher
5. Writing letters as they are drawn on a child's back

The following published items may be useful.*

Look workbooks or spirit masters (Macmillan)
Touch Teaching Alphabet (Child)
Tactile Letter Blocks (Child)
Rubber Stamp Alphabets (Child, CP, DX)
Vinyl Letters (OL, Child)
Tactile Alphabet Puzzles (Child)
Pencil Control Tracing Systems (Child, CP)
Wipe-Off Printing Book (Child)
Magic Tracks (Child)
Letter Tracing Stencils (Child, Lake, CP, DX)
Pencil Grips (Child, CP, DLM)
Transparent Shape Tracing Templates (EP, ETA)
Shape Stamps (DLM, CP, Lake, DX)
Kinesthetic Tracing Alphabet (CP)
Rol 'N Write, Letter Form Boards (CP, Lake)

---

*See page 57 for company names and addresses.

Overhead Projector Pattern Shapes in Colors (ETA)
Tactile Sandpaper Letters (DX)
Tactile Hardwood Letters (Lake)
Motor Letters (Lake)
Giant Tactile Letters (Lake)

TRAINING FORM PERCEPTION

Form perception is the ability to recognize, name, match, and remember objects, shapes, patterns, or symbols by the essential details of their form, shape, and other characteristics. It also involves the ability to appreciate that a basic shape or form, whether three- or two-dimensional, remains constant although it may vary in size, color, configuration, or orientation. It seems likely that even babies and young animals already possess a crude ability to recognize and respond to certain shapes and patterns.

For most children, much practice in form perception will have taken place in the preschool period as they played with toys and objects providing experiences in looking, manipulating, drawing, tracing, and cutting out. If they have been encouraged to talk about these activities with an adult, language of form will also have been acquired. This language experience will mean that such children begin school with ideas about different shapes and forms, their names, colors, sizes, and uses. In addition, if motor education has resulted in good body awareness and some appreciation of basic shapes, and if the child is not emotionally disturbed, then the child's response to teaching in school should be satisfactory.

Some children, however, need specific training in form perception. Perhaps all children benefit from such training at appropriate times and levels of development, particularly if language and classification are emphasized to achieve progress from perception *per se* to visual conceptualization (for example, "I am thinking of something which has six square sides all the same size. What is it?").

The following are suggested stages for a program of form perception training.

1. Developing language to enable naming, sorting, and classifying of toys, objects, shapes, etc.

2. Moving into and out of named shapes drawn on the floor or painted on the playground, walking, hopping around them, making shapes with the body or parts of the body

3. Recognizing different forms, and matching objects and shapes (for example, showing a form as a silhouette on the overhead projector and asking children to find it from a selection, and/or say what it is)

Using dominoes or lottoes

Using simple jigsaws and formboards

Fitting shapes or objects and geometric forms into stencils

4. Recognizing toys, objects, and shapes by haptic exploration (feeling with the eyes closed) and describing them in detail. This is an excellent activity for developing the language of form perception (for example, *long, short, thick, thin, hard, soft, rough, smooth, sharp, blunt, pointed, curved, sloping, big, little, top, bottom, middle, side*)

5. Identifying shapes, as when drawn on the child's back (as in sensory association work). Here again, expressive language can be effectively encouraged.

6. Making shapes and forms by experimenting with known shapes of different colors

7. Recognizing and identifying objects and shapes in different orientations (for example, as displayed on an overhead projector). This helps to establish ideas of form constancy.

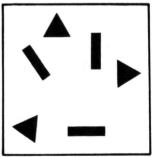

8. Recognizing shapes and objects in composite forms and pictures.

Activities 1 through 8 must eventually lead to recognition by form (and possibly sound) of letters, numerals, and words, if this total training in form perception is to result in hastening readiness for reading by a "look and say" approach, and early number activities. At this stage, too, training in position in space is important particularly in relation to the change in certain letters when rotated (for example, *b, d, p, q, u, n*). The overhead projector is a very useful aid for teaching position in space.

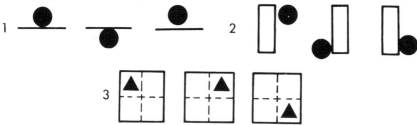

Examples such as those shown in the diagram can be used for teaching the language of position in space and the language of movement in space (for example, "I moved the little blue triangle from the top right-hand square to the bottom left-hand square."). The use and practice of this expressive language is also taught in the motor education programs.

The following are suggestions for further activities to train form perception.

1. Place an object or shape some inches away from the child and ask the child to choose the same thing from a selection in front of the child.
2. Filling in outline shapes
3. Using attribute blocks
4. Using pegboards to produce given shapes
5. Making patterns with tiles and cubes
6. Drawing and painting patterns
7. Sorting and classifying junk according to color, shape, size, material
8. Picture and shape dominoes
9. Bead stringing
10. Playing with graded sets of jigsaw puzzles of people and objects, preferably programmed by the teacher
11 Mosaic and matching games
12. Making shapes with rods, sticks, straws

Useful Materials for Training Form Perception*

Clear stencils (DLM)
Shape Sorters (DLM, OL, CP, Lake)
Shape Stamps (DLM, CP, Lake, DX)
Colored Cubes and Design Cards (DLM, ETA, Child, CP, Lake)
Stencil Shapes (OL)
Soft Shapes Alphabet (OL)
Large Parquetry Blocks and Design Cards (DLM, OL, Lake, ETA, Child, CP)
Locking Shapes (OL)
Attribute Blocks (Lake, OL, Child, CP)
Mr. Mighty Mind (OL)
Tactile Shape Puzzles (Lake, Child, CP)
Coordination Board (Lake, Child, CP)
Geo Form Board (Child, DX)
Color/Shape Abacus (Lake, Child, CP)
Magnetic Shapes (Child, Lake)
Color/Shape Bingo and Lotto (Child, Lake)
Colorama (Lake)
Shape and Color Matching Blocks (CP)
Geometric Dominoes (CP, Lake)
Cookie Monster Shape Muncher (CP)

TRAINING VISUAL DISCRIMINATION

Visual discrimination is a complex process, including form perception, position in space, sequencing, memory, and classification. It is the ability to appreciate differences and similarities in shape, form, color, pattern, size, sequential order, position, and orientation. Training this appreciation provides excellent opportunities for language development, particularly in relation to classification, and consequently to the development of concepts. This is fostered if the child is encouraged to talk about and discuss his reasons for selecting like and different objects, and so on.

The need for didactic teaching of visual discrimination varies between children, as does the need for teaching specific aspects of the total process. For example, some children appear to have difficulty in dealing with geometric shapes, but not with letters and words, and vice versa. Some display specific difficulties in discrimination involving orientation in space, while others have problems with

---

*See page 57 for company names and addresses.

differentiating patterns and sequences. For these reasons, the following suggestions should be used carefully if good learning habits and motivation are to result. Children should receive training in those parts of the program which they require. For all children, the ability to discriminate visually is improved by motor education which stresses visual-motor integration, left-right orientation, position in space, and sensory association work. This work, including the language development associated with it, should precede visual discrimination training at symbol level (1shape, letters, numerals, and words) or, in individual areas of difficulty, be carried out simultaneously. The important thing for teachers to remember is that discrimination and classification should be stressed in all early learning.

The following points are important when planning training in visual discrimination:

1. The language of same and different should be developed throughout.
2. Concrete objects (such as toys, counters, cubes, beads, books) should be used at first.
3. If appropriate, children should feel with their eyes closed (that is, haptic/visual association).
4. Children should be given wide experience of sorting and classifying according to color, shape, size, material, etc.
5. The overhead projector can be used in early recognition and matching work (for example, the children have a selection of animal shapes and select the one which is silhouetted on the screen). Begin with easy examples and proceed to the development of fine discrimination of shape, size, and orientation.
6. Repeat step 5 using various shapes. Plastic shapes are very useful, since the overhead projector can be used to discuss shape, size, and color, as in the following examples.

Same or different?

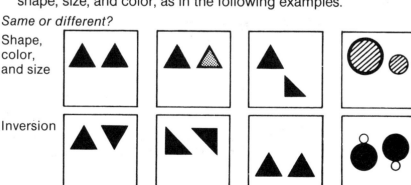

Shape, color, and size

Inversion

Rotation

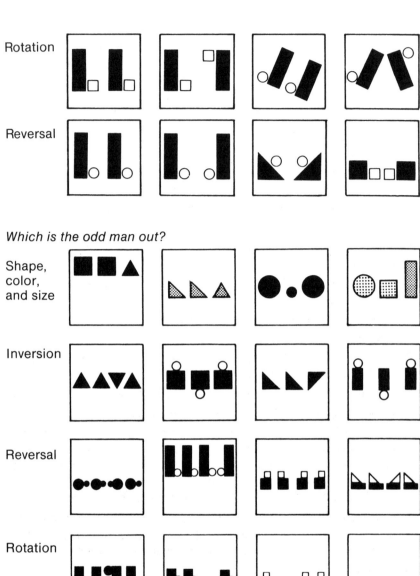

Reversal

Which is the odd man out?

Shape,
color,
and size

Inversion

Reversal

Rotation

Omission

7. Repeat the type of exercise in step 6, but use matchsticks, rods, or pipecleaners. In these exercises, use vertical and horizontal before slanting configurations.

Find the odd man out

⌐ L ⌐ I L ∧ ⟨ ∧∧

8. Again using the overhead projector, similar work can be done with individual cut-out letters, numbers, combinations of letters, and simple words, asking children if they are the same or different.

9. After work with the overhead projector, cards can be used for word matching games. Success at this level is an indication that the child's ability in visual discrimination is sufficient for the child to begin reading with a "look and say" approach. Most reading schemes have similar work in their prereading section. It is important to check that the programming is right for the child and that the later exercises give adequate training in recognition of similarities and differences in letters and in simple two- and three-letter words.

10. Left-handed children should normally be given more help in left-to-right orientation, rotation recognition, and visual and temporal sequencing (see page 34).

11. Teacher-made duplicated programs are often more valuable for individual children.

12. For children with learning difficulties, a multisensory approach is needed (for example, feeling letters made in sand, Plasticene, Play Dough, clay, pipe cleaners, or plastic) to differentiate same or different; putting letters into templates; saying whether a letter written on the back matches a visually displayed letter; saying when a letter written on the back matches the given letter.

Useful Materials for Training Visual Discrimination*

Overhead Projector Pattern Shapes in Colors (ETA)
Visual Perception Big Box (DLM)
Pre-Writing Design Cards (DLM)
Animals in Place (DLM)
Visual Perception Activity Masters (OL)
Find It Game (Child)
Lotto Games (all companies)
PerceptiSort (Child)
Color Paddles (Child, CP, Lake)
Same or Different Tiles (CP)
Wooden Difference Faces (CP)
Classifying Clues (CP)
Pre-Reading Discrimination Inset Boards (DX)
Simple Shapes Discovery Board (Lake)
Picture Silhouettes Lotto (Lake)

TRAINING VISUAL MEMORY AND SEQUENCING

Visual memory is the ability to recall a visual image of objects, forms, symbols, and movements. It plays a key role in all learning. It is to some degree a developmental process, but is also trainable, particularly in relation to its role in specific areas of learning or knowledge. It involves clear perception of what is seen, storage and retention of visual information, and its ready retrieval for use in comparing present with past visual experience, by which responses to the visual environment can be better organized and interpreted and thus contribute to total growth.

The development of efficient visual memory is dependent upon attention and concentration, keen observation, speed, and good motivation. These factors should be considered when planning training programs. Its relationship to other forms of memory (kinesthetic, auditory, and tactile) should also be remembered, particularly with children who appear to have poor memories. The role of language in labeling and fixing visual experience and in the development of visualization and visual imagery is also of fundamental importance.

Visual memory is a composite of different types of memory: short- and long-term, and sequential. Short-term visual memory is involved

---

*See page 57 for company names and addresses.

in activities such as the immediate recall of displayed material (for example, by tachistoscope) and in the more delayed recall, identification, and reproduction of shapes, forms, symbols, such as letters, words, and sentences, and recent visual experiences. Long-term memory is obviously very important in all learning and is concerned with retrieving visual images which are appropriate and relevant to new learning situations. In many instances, long-term memory has to be developed to the level of automatic response, as in acquiring a sight vocabulary.

Sequential memory of the order of letters in words and of words in sentences is an integral part of the visual decoding process in reading and the encoding process in spelling. Investigations into the reasons for reading and spelling failure have consistently revealed that poor visual sequencing skill is often involved. In any prereading program, therefore, training in visual sequencing would seem to be essential, particularly for children who already indicate that they have problems in body awareness, laterality and directionality, and awareness of spatial relationships. Regular, programmmed, and systematic teaching is desirable for these children.

The following activities have proved to be useful in training designed to improve visual memory. As in all aspects of training perception, programming of material is important.

Motor Activities

1. Copying a series of body movements either as demonstrated by the teacher or as shown on large cards

2. Remembering and walking movement patterns previously seen on a programmed set of cards

3. Moving to stand on different shapes varying in color and size (red square, blue circle, yellow diamond, etc.)

Memory Games

1. Randomly display two or three objects for a few seconds, then cover them and ask the child to name them. Over a period of time increase the number.

2. Using the overhead projector, let the children see for 5 to 10 seconds, two, three, or more shapes of objects or geometric forms randomly placed, then cover the image and ask children to name or draw the objects. This overhead projector work is most useful and can be developed by using transparent colored shapes.

Stage a: Use two similar shapes of the same color, then increase the number to involve counting with one-to-one correspondence.

Stage b: Use similar shapes of different colors.

Stage c: Use different shapes of the same color.

Stage d: Use different shapes of different colors.

Stage e: Use similar shapes of different sizes, but the same color.

Stage f: Use similar shapes of different colors and size.

Stage g: Use different shapes of different colors and size.

In all but the first stage, gradually increase the number of shapes displayed but ensure that the children can name the shapes and colors and can differentiate the sizes.

3. The work in step 2 can be done without the overhead projector, using toys, colored cubes and beads, familiar objects and pictures of toys and objects. Work on classification can also be incorporated by showing the children an object or shape, or groups of them, and then removing them from view, and asking the children to select from another set of objects and shapes those which belong to the same family, or which go with the one displayed. For example, briefly show a diamond shape and the children select all diamonds, show a cup and the children select saucers, show an item of clothing and the children select all other items of clothing, using attribute blocks, show a thick, big, yellow circle and the children choose shapes and say why they have chosen them.

4. On the overhead projector display a stimulus for two seconds and then ask the children to draw it, starting with one simple shape and then increasing the number of shapes or the complexity of one shape.

5. Make a shape with rods, matchsticks, or straws. Cover the shape and ask the children to make the shape.

6. All the above can later be repeated using letter shapes and words.

7. To increase speed of reaction, the overhead projector can be used to briefly expose an object (for example, a shape is shown for a second or less, and the children select or name the shape; later, two or three shapes or objects are flashed onto the screen.)

8. Show a group of five objects for five seconds, cover them and remove one, show the new group and ask children to identify

what is missing. Repeat by adding a new object or simply show and ask children what objects they saw. This game becomes more exciting if the overhead projector is used and the time of exposure varied.

9. Play a concentration game using sets of matching cards; one set is scattered face down and the children try to find the card which matches the one held.

10. Show a picture, a simple one at first, and ask the child to describe it in detail.

Activities for Training Memory of Visual Sequences and Developing Ideas of Order and Pattern

The ability to observe, recognize, remember, and reproduce sequences of symbols in words and sentences is a prerequisite for reading and spelling. The act of reading aloud involves the ability to transduce visual-spatial sequences into the audiotemporal sequences of speech. The reverse of this is involved in spelling. Training in sequencing skills and memory is crucial.

Training can begin with very young children by teaching them to remember two or three toys or objects in sequence. Later, pictures may be used and then geometric shapes. The overhead projector is invaluable in this work, particularly if transparent, colored plastic shapes are used. Sequences growing in length and complexity are shown for 5 to 10 seconds, and the children, using another set of shapes, attempt to reproduce the sequencing correctly. A training project could develop along the following lines:

STAGE	Ⓡ=red Ⓑ=blue Ⓖ=green Ⓨ=yellow
1	(R) (R) [B] [B] [B] ⬜G ⬜G ⬜G ⬜G
2	(R) (G) [Y] [B] △G △Y
3	(G) (Y) (R) [G] [R] [Y] [B] △G △Y △R △B
4	△R [R] [Y] (Y) △Y (G) [G] [G] △G
5	[R] (Y) (G) △B [R] [Y] △R (B) [G]
6	(B) Ⓑ (Y) ⬛B [Y] △R ⓖ △B ⓖ [Y] Ⓡ

This type of activity is popular with four- to six-year-old children, particularly if an element of challenge is introduced. Variations are the use of animal and toy shapes; flashcards of programmed shape and picture sequences instead of the overhead projector; stringing sequences of colored beads of different shapes, colors and sizes, from demonstrations with the beads or flashcards of bead sequences. Patterns of sequences can also be used.

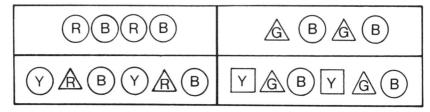

The above sequencing activities can be adapted for the training of auditory sequencing (see page 43). The teacher gives sequences orally for the children to repeat verbally and reproduce visually or by drawing. Indeed, in training visual-motor sequencing teachers should use language extensively. The objects, shapes, and forms used should be described and named, developing the language of shape, color, size, position, and use.

Teachers should also note the importance of recognizing, memorizing, and reproducing sequences and patterns in mathematics. For example, seriating objects, shapes, or groups according to size is basically a process of ordering and patterning.

Activities for Training Memory of Position and Movement in Space

These must follow the training already mentioned. Using the overhead projector or teacher-made cards, the children practice remembering the position of objects based on ideas of *top, bottom, left, right, inside, center, opposite, diagonal, above, below, on, under, near, far, touching, overlapping.* The teacher prepares cards or duplicated sheets for the children to use in placing objects in the correct, memorized positions. The material must be programmed from very simple to quite complex arrangements.

Teachers should ensure that the children can also accurately describe the position of the objects or shapes (for example, "on the line and in the middle," "in the top, right-hand corner"). Further practice can be given by asking for exact details of the position of things in simple, and later, more complex pictures. Drawing simple maps of the school or home environment is another useful variation.

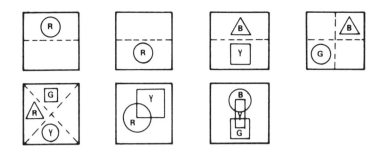

Training in visual-motor activity, when movements are memorized, has already been mentioned. The act of writing is based on visual and kinesthetic memory and for some children training is necessary. This may include moving shapes on an overhead porjector and then asking children to repeat from memory using shapes and a square piece of card, or drawing on the chalkboard for the children to reproduce from memory. The teacher writes a word on a card, the child traces over the word with the first finger, moves some distance and tries to write the word from memory. The tracing is repeated until accuracy is achieved; the child comparing each attempt until accuracy is achieved.

Most of the above activities involve the use of two-dimensional material, but three-dimensional material should also be used in order to develop perceptual abilities involved in translating two-dimensional representations into three-dimensional form.

The various aspects of visual retention and recall have been dealt with at some length because of their fundamental role in all academic pursuits and in life generally. In association with language and extended into the realms of visual imagery and imagination, they aid the development of thought and creative activity. Young children should be encouraged in the development of visualization, by asking such questions as, "How can I make this rectangle into a house? This is half a picture, what is the whole picture like?"

Useful Materials for Training Visual Memory and Sequencing*

Visual Sequential Memory Exercises (DLM)
Visual Memory Cards I-IV (DLM)
Visual Matching, Memory and Sequencing Exercises (DLM)
Sequence (CC)
Sequence Puzzles (Lake, CP, Child)
Memory Games (CP, Child)
Sequence Shapes (Child)
Rainbow Towers (CP)
Sequencing Sizes (Lake, CP)
Visual Recall Cards (CP)
Sequence and Rhythm Boards (DX)
Shadow Picture Memory Game (Lake)
Now You See It, Now You Don't (Lake)
Hardwood Memory Tiles (Lake)
Complete the Pattern Game (Lake)
Step-by-Step Memory Game (Lake)
Easy as 1, 2, 3 (CS)

TRAINING VISUAL RHYTHM

Training in visual patterns and rhythm are included in perceptual training because of their apparent importance in encouraging children to develop sequential anticipation in reading, expressive language, and thought. Writing is concerned with rhythmic, flowing fine movements involving what has been called the "kinetic melody," that is, the control of excitation and inhibition in movement at the automatic level.

The program of training visual rhythm should include the following:

1. Developing the language of movement, line, dot, cross, circle, up, down, etc. in anticipation of the handwriting program

2. Continuing patterns using whole body positions and movements (for example, one child sits, one stands, one kneels, and children then repeat the sequence)

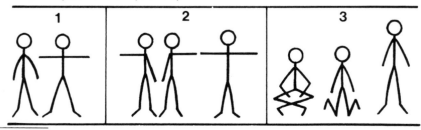

*See page 57 for company names and addresses.

3. Continuing patterns using rods, beads, colored cubes

4. Continuing patterns in finger painting, perhaps using auditory rhythms to encourage integrated auditory, motor, and visual rhythm

5. Continuing rhythms either shown on cards or on prepared duplicated sheets, beginning with simple rhythms and progressing to more complex ones

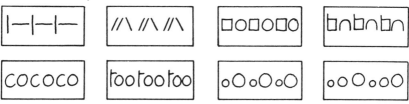

6. Writing patterns related to the writing program (see page —)

Throughout this training, children should be encouraged to talk and thus realize the association between auditory, vocal, visual, and motor rhythm sequences (for example, *small big, big small... up and down, down and up...*).

TRAINING VISUAL CLOSURE AND COMPLETION

The ability to "close" a figure in the absence of part of it appears to be significant in reading and perceptual activities generally. Reading with speed while at the same time maintaining accuracy involves closure. Speedy identification of objects, people, shapes, forms, and configurations in the environment and pictures also depends upon visual closure, when often responses are made by "closing" incomplete representations or by referring to significant details only (for example, lines, corners, angles, gradients in light and shade). It would seem desirable to give some training in the speedy identification of "wholes" in the absence of parts of them.

Incomplete pictures, preferably drawn by the teacher, in which only parts of the objects or actions are revealed, are valuable, not only for training in closure but also for language development. Incomplete figures or patterns are presented on individual cards. The children point to, trace over, or say what is missing. They may also choose the missing part from a selection.

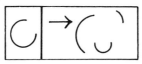 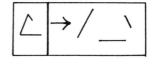

Many children's books and comics often include pictures with hidden objects in them (for example, "How many animals can you find in this picture?"). Joining dots to make pictures, completing jigsaw puzzles, finishing incomplete drawings in a free way, and building three-dimensional models from cubes, cuboids, cylinders, cones are additional activities for training in visual closure and completion.

TRAINING VISUAL TEMPORAL SEQUENCING

Visual temporal sequencing is concerned with appreciating the order in time of experiences, letters in words, words in sentences, and stages in logical problem solving. It is, of course, closely related to form perception, visual sequencing and discrimination. The following activities are suggested to provide training.

1. Programmed sets of picture cards depicting a story or an event. The children arrange the cards in the right time order to tell a logical story and then relate the story in words. The number of cards in a story should be gradually increased from two to, say, ten (for example, a baby growing up to an old person, a flower in stages of development from a seed, making a cup of tea, a day in a child's life, making a cake). Arranging things into an ordered sequence according to size or number should also be included, as well as reverse order

2. Arranging cards of diagrams and patterns in various stages of completion

3. Using more complicated picture sequences involving high levels of logical thought, similar to those picture arrangement items used in nonverbal intelligence tests

4. Valuable language and memory work can arise from these activities. The following words should be learned thoroughly: *first, second, third, last, middle, after, before, next, earlier, later, sooner, begin, end, beginning, ending, left, right, winter, spring, summer, autumn*

5. For memory training, the child should be asked to tell the complete story from memory when the pictures have been correctly placed in temporal sequence. This provides invaluable training in sentence structure and the ordering of sentences into paragraphs.

Useful Materials for Teaching Visual Closure/ Visual Temporal Sequencing*

Figure-Ground Activity Cards (DLM)
Visual Closure Cards (OL)
Size and Shape Formboards (OL, CP, Lake)
What's Next (Child)
Time and Growth Cards (CS, Child, CP)
Hidden Objects Cards (CP)
Designs and Lines (CP)
Montessori Cylinder Blocks (CP, DX, Lake)
Nesting Toys (Child, CP, DX, Lake)
Seriation Flannelboard Figures (CP)
Silhouette Dominoes (CP)
Visual Inset Trays (DX)
Color Coded Sentence Building Kit (DX)
Complete the Picture Lotto (Lake)
Temporal Sequence Cards (DLM, Lake)
Part/Whole Lotto (Lake)

TRAINING IN FIGURE-GROUND RELATIONSHIPS

Some perceptual training programs include activities for training in figure-ground relationships, working on the view that children with poor figure-ground discrimination have difficulty in extracting meaning from the visual environment and pictures, and in attending to individual words on a page. They cannot distinguish individual items from the background in which they are embedded. This seems to be a difficulty for very few children, possibly due to neuromotor problems, and may be a reason for their distractibility and difficulties in moving safely and economically in space.

A good motor education program and training in visual perception along the lines detailed above appears to help children with figure-ground problems, particularly if language and speech are emphasized. However, they may need specific help using the following activities.

---

*See page 57 for company names and addresses.

1. Identifying a named object or shape from groups of increasing size
2. Identifying according to color and size
3. Pointing to named objects or shapes in pictures, starting with simple pictures and progressing to more complex ones
4. Moving a named object in space
5. Tracing, drawing round or coloring named objects or shapes in a picture or diagram
6. Working with shapes and overlapping them and identifying overlapped shapes in pictures. Transparent shapes can be used for this purpose, since the covered parts do not disappear and can be identified by changes in color and shade; the overhead projector is particularly useful in this context.

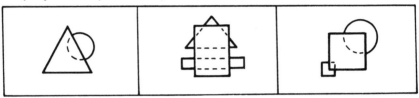

7. Playing with shadow puppets and talking about which is in front or behind as relative positions change
8. Using duplicated material prepared by the teacher, coloring seen or partly hidden shapes or things
9. Later on, finding words or sentences on a page, or circling letters asked for out of a collection (for example, "Circle all the e's: a, e, f, e, g, y, e)
10. Working on mazes of gradually increasing complexity
11. Working with programmed sets of jigsaw puzzles, starting with pictures of simple, clearly defined objects and working toward more complex figures with detailed backgrounds

Different aspects of visual perception training have been discussed, but their relationship to each other and to motor and language development must be stressed. Training in all areas should be simultaneous and every opportunity of training perception in all curriculum areas should be taken. It is essential that all teachers in the school involved with particular groups of children should know about and use perceptual training ideas and activities. Specialist teachers of movement, art, craft, and music can make a significant contribution to the perceptual development of children which will lead to the enhancement of general growth and learning in basic subjects.

Training Auditory Perception

Auditory perception is a process which involves hearing, listening, identifying, discriminating, interpreting, retaining, and retrieving auditory stimuli. It is an essential factor in all learning and particularly in reading and language development. However, the role of auditory perception in different aspects of learning varies according to the relative contributions of the specific auditory perception skills involved. The auditory skills involved in gaining facility in expressive and receptive language are largely the same as those used in learning to read. It should follow that young children with good language development should experience little difficulty in learning to read. This correlation is not always the case. Expressive language ability in fact does not always appear to be a good predictor of possible success in reading, and many reading failures have no outstanding difficulty with language usage. They have rich receptive language vocabularies and can communicate quite well, and this anomaly means that a language experience approach to teaching the beginning of reading may not always be successful. One important reason for this lack of correlation is the motor and visual perception content in reading, and it seems that reading success depends on good visual and auditory integration. Also of importance is the more sophisticated use of certain subskills in auditory perception—being sensitive to and identifying and discriminating between letter sounds, memorizing the sequences of sounds, blending or "closing" individual sounds in a smooth rhythmic way in correct temporal order to make words. Observations over many years appear to confirm that children who have good recognition of beginnings and endings in words, and of individual letter sounds or syllables in spoken words, are likely to make good progress in early reading.

Training in auditory perception has been somewhat neglected and the following programs have been designed to make amends. Teachers should make sure that the child has no hearing defect. Most children soon after entering school will be tested by audiometer, but it is still important for teachers to watch for any signs of impaired hearing, such as general inattentiveness or vagueness, failure to follow simple directions, frequent requests for repetitions of instructions, frequent colds and upper-respiratory infections, indistinct speech and consonantal substitutions, particularly of sounds like *f* and *th, sh* and *ch,* final *d* and *t.*

The importance of developing good listening habits must be stressed. Children often live in an atmosphere of so much noise that they have limited experience of quiet conversation, and do not feel the need to listen for significance in sound. In such circumstances they become expert in "switching off" or not listening. They later have difficulty in auditory figure-ground differentiation (that is, they cannot pick out and attend to sounds mixed in a background of general noise, as in a busy classroom).

Listening is *more* than hearing. It incorporates discrimination, interpretation, long- and short-term memory, acceptance or rejection (as in auditory figure-ground discrimination), and understanding and comprehension at various levels, literal, inferential, and critical. One of the benefits of training in auditory perception is improvement in listening skills and attention span, leading to improved comprehension.

TRAINING AUDITORY DISCRIMINATION

The following games and activities are recommended for training auditory discrimination.

Listening

Listening to stories read or told by the teacher or prerecorded. If stories on cassette are used the children should be asked to do something at the end of the story (for example, draw a picture or answer prerecorded questions).

Identifying Sound

1. Listening with eyes closed, and identifying sounds, either visually or in the classroom, playground, and general environment

2. Using prerecorded sounds and pictures, matching sounds to pictures. This should be programmed to increase in difficulty over a period of time.

3. With eyes closed, identifying different objects as they are dropped onto a table (pencil, coin, book, etc.), or shaken (full matchbox, money box, bell, etc.)

4. Counting how many taps are made by a pencil on a table, or how many times a ball is bounced, or a triangle is hit. (This depends upon the ability to count with a one to one correspondence.)

5. Relating animal sounds to pictures and plastic models of animals

6. Playing "What is happening?" Sounds which relate to an event are made by the teacher (or a child) and the children discuss what happened. Begin with one or two sounds and gradually extend.

7. Taking the children on a listening expedition, recording sounds, discussing and getting children to suggest or create words to fit them (for example, screech of brakes, buzzing of bees, crunch of footsteps on gravel, whine of a car engine, rustle of leaves)

8. Using musical instruments, show and play the instruments, then play one behind a screen and ask the children to identify the instrument

9. Playing "Who is speaking?" The children, with eyes closed, identify a classmate who is speaking. Recorded voices of well-known people may also be used.

Sound Intensity

1. Using the voice or musical instruments, ask children to differentiate between louder and softer sounds

2. Playing games in which a blindfolded child is guided to an object by the clapping of the other children—the louder the clapping the nearer the child is to the object

3. Using two sets of boxes or cylinders which are all the same in appearance but containing nails, pebbles, peas, rice, sand, etc. The children pair them according to intensity of sound by shaking the boxes. Starting with two boxes and gradually increasing to five or six, children can seriate the sounds from softest to loudest, and loudest to softest. (Use the language of *first, second, middle, last, before, after.*) This seriating task can be combined with visual seriation (for example, "What color is the loudest box?"). Use boxes or cylinders with varying shades of the same color so that gradients in color match the gradients in sound intensity (for example, the darkest red might go with the loudest sound). The size of the boxes may also seriate in direct or opposite relationship to the sound seriation.

4. Practicing relating sound to movement (for example, whispering to gentle steps and shouting to heavy ones, shouting to high jumps and whispering to low ones). Play the scale on a piano or xylophone, starting with a loud note and gradually decreasing up or down the scale.

5. Playing simple pulse rhythms with accents (for example, loud, soft, loud, soft, loud, soft)

6. Playing recorded sounds of trains, airplanes, and cars to establish the relationship between soft sounds meaning far away and loud sounds meaning near. Also, that if the sound is getting louder the object is approaching, and if it is getting softer the object is moving away.

7. Using instruments, recordings, etc. to teach the relationship between sounds getting louder and getting softer

Training in Pitch

1. Using graded exercises, practice detecting variations in pitch, starting with large differences and going on to small variations

2. Playing or singing three notes to teach lowest, middle, and highest pitch, again decreasing the intervals

3. Playing "finding the object" (as in 2 above), but this time using changes in pitch to give the clues

4. Demonstrating pitch variations on piano, violin, guitar, showing high notes getting even higher and low notes getting lower

5. Reading or telling stores, using high and low voices as appropriate to individual characters (for example, The Three Bears)

6. Combine sound intensity and pitch by discussing environmental sounds, perhaps previously recorded, by asking such questions as "Which sound was the loudest?"

7. Combine visual and pitch patterns, using patterns such as:

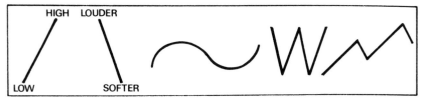

8. Combine movements with pitch (for example, stretching for high and squatting for low sounds

Training in Sound Duration

1. Combining children's movements with sound duration (for example, long step, short step)
2. Establishing relationships, such as high is loud and long, low is soft and short
3. Discussing popular tunes with regard to variations in duration of notes or chords
4. Speaking simple rhythms, or playing them on instruments or buzzer board

Training Fine Auditory Discrimination

To ensure that auditory discrimination is sufficiently developed to assist in the acquisition of reading and communication skills, it must have reached a level where it deals with discrimination of letter sounds and words. The following activities are suggested for this prephonic work.

1. Clapping when a given word is heard in a collection of words
2. Clapping when a word for a flower, color, shape, etc. is heard in a collection of words (for example, "Clap when you hear a word for a shape—man, square, blue, oblong.")
3. Discussing the sounds made when a person sighs or sneezes, or pretends to be a bee, a pig, a dog, a cat, or blows out a candle, or wants somebody to be quiet, etc.
4. Identifying pairs of words which are the same or different (for example, sat—sit, chip—chip, ship—chip, seat—seek, chair—cheer, etc.). This work might be prerecorded for cassette listening, the child putting a check mark or a cross in the boxes for same and different (for example, "Put a check mark or a cross in box 1 for these two words: *back—bank*. Now for box 2: *they—day*.).
5. Identifying words which end with the same sound. For most consonants, the correct phonic sound is heard at the end of words, not at the beginning (for example, sit—cat, man—tin—begin, trick—track). Further training in identification of words ending in the same sound can be provided by asking children to select from a prepared collection of pictures or objects, or riddles such as, "I am an animal and my name ends with the sound t ('t' as in sit, not 'tuh')." "I am a color and my name ends in d."

6. Identifying words which begin with the same sound,
   a. Give a word and identify its initial sound, then ask children to indicate when a given word begins with the same sound (for example, mouse—my, garden, mother, marmalade, jumping).
   b. Collect pictures for children to classify according to initial sounds.
   c. I spy something beginning with . . .
   d. Find the stranger in a collection of pictures or drawings of objects, all but one beginning with the same sound.
   e. Use picture and sound dominoes.
   f. Play alliteration games gradually extending the number of words used.

7. Identifying middle sounds. This is often difficult for young children with learning difficulties, and requires practice. Indeed, it might be advisable to omit this aspect of sound identification if the child shows signs of frustration. "What sound is in the middle of these words: *sitting, cutting, writing?*" Confusion can arise through using some words for this work (for example, *man, mat, map*). Teachers may want the children to identify the short vowel sound *a,* but it might be better to teach that *man, mat, map* begin with *ma.* This is particularly so when words begin with a plosive sound (for example, *bat, cat, dot, got, pot, top*).

8. Recognition of final, initial, and middle sounds can be practiced by asking the children to indicate the position of sounds in words (for example, "Where do you hear the *m* sound in these words: *my, ham, coming, mum, mummy?*"). This work is useful in helping children to blend and appreciate audio-temporal sequencing.

9. Identifying words which rhyme, using pictures, riddles, snap and bingo. Nursery rhymes for younger children and simple poems are useful when a rhyming word has to be identified to complete a line. Many children like to make up their own poems selecting their own rhyming words.

In the activities listed in 5 to 9, teaching children to identify or write the actual letters is valuable, if they are ready. For children who have already acquired a stock of sight words, it is extremely helpful to use these words for fine auditory discrimination work and for prephonic work. Picture dictionaries and alphabetic lists of known words should be made, thus emphasizing sight-symbol relationship and identification by initial sounds.

TRAINING AUDITORY MEMORY AND SEQUENCING

The following activities are useful in training memory and developing ideas of sound and conceptual sequencing.

1. Choosing two or more named items from a collection of objects, first with eyes open, and then closed while the items are named

2. Giving the children three or more pictures to look at and then place face-down. Describe one, then ask that a certain picture be found. This can be programmed to a level where the children are dealing with shapes, colors, letters, and words (from known sight vocabulary).

3. Extend activity 1 to reproduction of sequences, starting with two items to be placed in the correct order, and extending eventually to five or six.

4. Use exercises given in *Motor Education* (Tansley 1986) in which movements are described for the children to execute from memory.

5. Repeating well-known sequences (for example, numbers, days of the week, months of the year). Vary this by asking children to indicate when part of a sequence is out of order (for example, Monday, Tuesday, Wednesday, Friday).

6. Remembering nursery rhymes, jingles, simple poems, hymns

7. Following simple instructions, gradually extended, when heard once. Repeat this activity with a delay of 10 to 15 minutes, or longer.

8. Retelling a story in the correct order or, when the story has been heard, answering a question posed at the beginning

9. Describing a television program seen the previous evening

10. Playing the shopping game. The first child says, "I went to the grocery store and bought some apples." The second child repeats this and adds another purchase, and so on.

11. Similar to activity 10, but using nonsense words (for example, *brug, nast, lang*)

12. Describing in correct time order how to make a cup of tea or a cake

13. Repeating a sequence of sounds made by different musical instruments, shakers, bells, etc. of varying size and pitch

14. Using a triangle or xylophone and striking two, three, or more notes as given orally

15. Repeating a series of numbers, up to six forward and four backward

16. Remembering and counting how many claps or taps heard, how many words in sentences, or letters in words given orally

There are other activities which will improve auditory memory and sequencing. Since poor short-term auditory memory and defective ideas of order seem to be common among poor readers, training is important. It need not be as didactic as suggested above for some children, but children's ability to memorize should be challenged regularly in many areas of school activity.

TRAINING AUDITORY RHYTHM

Investigations into reasons for failure in phonic analysis and synthesis have revealed a relationship with poor rhythmic ability. Suggestions for developing a good sense of rhythm are given in *Motor Education* (Tansley 1986). Activities combining movement, music, and rhythm and asking children to talk as they move rhythmically are invaluable. Experience suggests that there is a close relationship between short-term auditory memory and ability to repeat spoken or tapped rhythms.

Rhythmic activities should be used to strengthen auditory memory and to develop a sense of temporal order. The following classroom activities should be used to reinforce and supplement rhythm work done in movement and music lessons.

1. Clapping or tapping rhythms demonstrated by the teacher, beginning with regular beats and going on to irregular rhythms

2. Saying rhythms as said or tapped, using "dah" and "di" (for example, __ __ . __ is dah-dah-di-dah)

3. Repeating 2, but children close their eyes or cannot see when the rhythms are said or tapped

4. Repeating 2 and 3, using a buzzer board to send Morse code type signals

5. Relating heard rhythms to visual representations (for example, the teacher taps, says, or sings "dah-dah-di-di-dah-dah" and the children select the correct visual pattern from the cards)

6. Extending 5 to the level when the children hear a rhythm and write out the visual representation using dots and dashes, or other symbols. It is useful to train the children to then say and tap the rhythms simultaneously. Failure to do this auditory-motor-vocal integration task may indicate possible difficulties in phonics, particularly in the rhythmic blending of sounds.

7. Tapping a rhythm which the children identify when tapped again

TRAINING AUDITORY CLOSURE

The skill of blending sounds together to make words is fundamental to effective reading and involves all the auditory perception skills: listening, fine auditory discrimination, auditory short-term memory, auditory sequencing and rhythm, differentiating significant sounds from background noise, and auditory closure. The teaching of phonics has to aim at making closures speedily—in many cases automatically—so that most words are eventually read almost as sight words. The use of context clues in phonics (for example, using meaning to decipher a strange word) is dependent on the closure or Gestalt process.

The following activities will be useful in training auditory closure.

1. Guessing words when only parts are given (for example, thinking of an animal whose name begins with *ra, do,* or *hipp*). Name endings and middle sounds should also be used.

2. Extending 1 to include rhymes (for example, thinking of an animal whose name begins with *chimp* and rhymes with *tree*)

3. Playing word games (such as, "Think of three words with the sound *all* in them, *at* in them." "Think of three words which end with *ank, tion, ful.")*

4. Asking the child to count or tap how many sounds or syllables there are in words

5. Asking the child to identify the sounds in words (for example, *air-plane, el-e-phant*)

6. Asking the child to identify a word when a sound or sounds are missing (for example, *ca-van, f-mer, ta-recor-*)

7. How many words can you think of which begin with *ma, ski, dis?*

8. Giving individual letter sounds or phonemes for the children to blend into words which they already know. In teaching reading at the early phonic stage, this oral blending should usually be done before words are encountered visually.

TRAINING IN AUDITORY
FIGURE-GROUND DISCRIMINATION

Training in auditory figure-ground discrimination normally has to be done by using prerecorded material, the aim being to help the children to pay attention to words, music, or instructions which have to be picked out of background noise, as is usually the case in the everyday environment. For example, in an active classroom, the child has to attend to the teacher's voice against a background of noise and conversation. Auditory figure-ground problems are probably not present for most children. Teachers should remember that some children have serious difficulties in this auditory process, even when their auditory acuity is normal. For all children, having to learn in a noisy, confused atmosphere can be very tiring. Opportunities should be provided for quiet times. The use of taped lessons can be useful because, using headphones, the child can listen to stories or teaching material which is completely free from background noise and interference. Story time and listening to soothing music are also helpful.

For children with normal hearing who show signs of auditory figure-ground confusion, such as restlessness, poor attention, or a need for frequent repetition of instructions or questions, the following suggestions will be useful.

1. Using prerecorded material, starting at first with several teaching sessions with no background noise. Over a period of time, gradually increase the background noise or sounds (for example, the sound of a vacuum cleaner, soft music, or quiet classroom background sounds). Difficulties can be expected when the background noise is about 10 decibels below the significant sound. Normal children can usually cope when the background noise is at the same level as the significant sounds, or even up to 5 decibels above.

2. Sitting the children near to the teacher, or in free group and play situations, going close to the child when speaking

3. Asking the child to listen to specific sounds in the environment

4. Clearly articulating the child's name when calling for him to listen

5. In some situations, as in a gymnasium where echo is bad, or outside, the teacher should pay particular attention to figure-ground problems.

DEVELOPING AUDITORY IMAGERY

The section on Training Visual Perception briefly mentioned the need for visual perception to lead to visualization. Visualization of spatial relationships and patterns seems to be particularly important. One of the principal differences between physical and motor education is that the latter deals with motor patterns and spatial concepts. The word *visualization* can refer to nonvisual stimuli, as in visualizing smell, touch, and sounds. Very little is known about this in developing strategies for learning, but any program for developing auditory perception and processes should include work involving auditory imagery, if only for the language experience it can provide.

The following activities will help children to develop auditory imagery.

1. Using prerecorded sound pictures for the children to describe what is happening, beginning simply (for example, with the sound of footsteps in gravel, and building up to more complex situations)

2. A picture or silent film is shown and the children select from two or more recordings one which fits the picture or film.

3. Playing two or three pieces of music for the children to select the most appropriate piece to fit a particular picture or film

4. In free drama work, discussing with the children the type of background noise or music which might be suitable

5. Asking the children to describe sounds of the countryside, the town, the seaside, etc.

Useful Materials for Teaching Auditory Skills

Musical Instruments
Boxes containing pebbles, rice, beans, nails, buttons, sand, etc.
Collection of pictures, shapes, toys, colored beads, counters, and
　　cubes for memory and sequencing work
Teacher-made Morse Code type cards
Teacher-made picture cards for final, initial, and middle sounds
Cassette players and audio activity center
Headphones
Sound effects records
Recorded music for atmosphere in drama

Comprehensive Programs*
APT: Auditory Perceptive Training (DLM)
Auditory Discrimination in Depth (DLM)
Listen, Speak, Read, and Spell (DLM)
Auditory Memory for Language (CC)
Auditory Discrimination Training Program (CC)
Tutorette Audio Card Programs (ABC)

Other books and materials
What's That I Hear? (CS)
Sound Investments (CS)
Sounds in My World (CS)
Sounds the Same (CS)
Sound Stories (CS)
Learn to Listen (CS, CP)
Sound/Picture Match-Ups (DLM)
Auditory Familiary Sounds (DLM)
Building Auditory and Visual Perception Skills (OL)
Listening and Following Directions Cassettes (OL, Lake)
Time to Rhyme Activity Masters (OL)
Sounds Lotto (Child)
Listen and Match (Child)
Simon and Pocket Simon (Child, CP, Lake)
Rhyming Bingo (Child, Lake)
Sound Cylinders (CP, Lake)
Pictures that Rhyme (flannelboard) (CP)
I'm All Ears Activity Cards (CP, Lake)
Auditory Closure Cards (CP)
Listen and Learn Lotto (CP)
Touch and Tell (CP)
Matching Sounds Cylinders (DX)
Lotto I, II (Lake)
Developing Listening Skills, Masters (Lake)

---

*See page 57 for company names and addresses.

Using the Overhead Projector
in Perceptual Training

The overhead projector is an invaluable aid in perceptual training and certainly stimulates motivation and attention. It is particularly useful for group work and in developing the language of perception and classification. The following suggestions show some of the many ways in which it can be used.

1. Show common objects (for example, pen, coins, scissors, keys) as silhouettes on the screen and ask the children to identify them.

2. Let the children see you draw around a silhouette. Remove the object to reveal the outline. Allow children to draw around objects and see consequent shapes. Talk about the forms to develop ideas of line, curve, angle, corner, shape, etc.

3. Use prepared transparencies of outlines of objects, plastic toys, shapes, and forms and ask the children to find the corresponding item from their collection and fit it into the outline on the transparency or screen. A program of transparencies can be made to develop skills in matching, orientation, position in space, size variation, and seriation.

4. Use colored transparent shapes for the children to identify by color, shape, and size. Use the shapes for the following perceptual training activities.

Form Perception
Making forms out of combinations of the shapes.

Figure-Ground Relationships
Overlap the shapes and ask the children to identify the individual shapes used, or ask questions such as "How many triangles can you find?" Teach color and shade change when different colors overlap.

Visual Discrimination
Teach differences between shapes, colors, sizes and identifying shapes in different orientations.

Position in Space

Place one or more shapes in different positions and ask the children to describe the position accurately. Use prepared grids and ask children to place shapes in the same position as shown on the screen, then repeat from memory. Change the position of a shape and then ask the children to describe what happened, or put the shape back and ask a child to repeat the movement on the overhead projector.

Visual Memory and Sequencing

Use the shapes to train visual memory for sequences of up to six items varying color, shape, and size.

Closure

Using lines and shapes, construct partly completed shapes or pictures and ask the children to complete them. Examples follow.

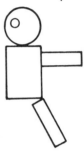

Visual Copying

Ask children to copy what you make on the screen, either by using the shapes or drawing. Repeat from memory.

Auditory Memory and Sequencing

Ask a child to follow instructions and make a figure, shape, or sequence on the overhead projector (for example, "In a line first put a big red circle, next a blue triangle, then a small yellow square, and last, a long thin green rectangle."). The other children can check the response. Alternatively, the other children could use shapes to make the sequence on a card. Cover the display and ask the children to give the sequence orally.

Ask the children to point to shapes in a given order (for example, "First point to a blue triangle, then a green square, and last, a little red circle.").

1. Visual perception work can also be done using matchsticks, straws, pipe cleaners, string, or letter shapes, for copying,

drawing, language work, closure and completion. Figure-ground work can be done by making the displays against increasingly distracting backgrounds previously prepared on transparencies.

2. Set and classification work, also involving form perception, using objects in silhouette and shapes

3. Use the overhead projector as a tachistoscope (that is, to give a brief, measured exposure of an object to the eye) to hasten responses in visual recognition and memory. Displays should be covered by a card after increasingly shorter exposures.

4. Auditory training (for example, "Find something on the screen whose name ends with the sound *t,* begins with the sound *m*")

After using the overhead projector for a short time, its immense potential as an aid to training and education in movement, perception, language, and thinking will be appreciated. It can be used as a basic training medium, after which children can be directed to published or teacher-made materials for further practice and reinforcement.

Reference

Tansley, A. E. 1986. *Motor Education.* Tucson, AZ: Communication Skill Builders.

Record Keeping

This suggested record sheet has been included as a guide to teachers who wish to keep a simple record of children's progress through the visual and auditory perception training programs.

SENSORY ASSOCIATION

Vision	normal	slightly defective	very defective
Hearing	normal	slightly defective	very defective

Hearing sweep test result _____ Date _____

Visual/auditory

Points to correct answer on hearing names of

pictures	☐
common shapes	☐
letters	☐
words	☐

Gives correct name when shown

pictures	☐
common shapes	☐
letters	☐
words	☐

Visual/Kinesthetic

Child is blindfolded when teacher holds his hand and draws in the air. When blindfold is removed, child can then select correct tiems from a visual display of

common shapes	☐
letters	☐
3 letter words	☐

Child is shown a shape, letter, or word, and then indicates when the same item is drawn on his back.

common shapes	☐
letters	☐
3 letter words	☐

Visual/Haptic

Having been shown an object or letter, child can identify the same item from a selection of three by touch and movement only, using a bag or screen.

toys	☐
common shapes	☐
letters	☐
(plastic, cut-outs, sand on glue, etc.)	

Child feels an object or letter out of sight in a bag or
behind a screen, and can identify it from a visual display of
three.   toys   □
                  common shapes □
                  letters   □
                  (as above)

Visual/motor
Can copy   □

Can draw from memory   □

Motor/vocal
Child can touch thumb tip with individual finger tips and count from
1 to 4 simultaneously.   □

VISUAL PERCEPTION
Ocular Pursuit
Good   □
Average   □
Poor   □

Hand-eye coordination
1 cm tracks completed   □
5 cm tracks completed   □
Catches a ball thrown from 3 meters, 4 out of 6 tries   □
Writing program completed
    with line and color cues   □
    without lines cues   □
    without color cues   □
    copies letters and words accurately   □

Form perception
Can name common objects   □
        toys   □
        animals   □
        shapes   □

Can match shapes   □
        letters   □
        simple words   □

Can copy stick patterns   □

Human body jigsaw puzzles
        4 pieces   □
        8 pieces   □
        10 pieces   □

Picture jigsaw puzzles
    8 pieces   □
    12 pieces   □
    16+ pieces   □

Copies accurately   □

○ □ ✕ △ □ ◇ ◇ ⊠

Visual Memory and Sequencing
Draws from memory   □

○ □ ✕ △ □ ◇ ◇ ⊠

Write first name from memory   □
Writes surname from memory   □

Reproduces after 10 seconds exposure
2️⃣ 3️⃣ 4️⃣ 5️⃣ 6️⃣ pictures in correct sequence

2️⃣ 3️⃣ 4️⃣ 5️⃣ 6️⃣ shapes in correct sequence

2️⃣ 3️⃣ 4️⃣ 5️⃣ 6️⃣ graphemes in correct sequence

Temporal sequencing
Places 2️⃣ 3️⃣ 4️⃣ 5️⃣ 6️⃣ pictures in correct temporal order

AUDITORY PERCEPTION
Speech   normal   slightly defective   defective

Listening Skills
Can count 3️⃣ 4️⃣ 5️⃣ 6️⃣ taps unseen

Attention: good □   average □   poor□

Sound intensity
Seriated sound boxes 2️⃣ 3️⃣ 4️⃣ 5️⃣ 6️⃣

Pitch
Differentiates high and low sounds   □
                 octave interval   □
                 full tone interval   □
                 semi-tone interval   □

Rhythm
Can march in time with rhythm   □
Can march and count in time   □
Can remember, sing, and tap simultaneously

━ ● ━ ━ □   ━ ● ━ ● ━ □

● ● ━ ━ ━ □   ● ● ━ ━ ● ● ━ □

Auditory Short-Term Memory and Sequencing

Can repeat digits forward   3 digits ☐   4 digits ☐   5 digits ☐
                                          6 digits ☐

Can repeat digits in reverse order   2 digits ☐   3 digits ☐   4 digits ☐

Can touch thumb with individual finger tips and say simultaneously

                               lion, elephant, monkey, tiger   ☐
                               Mary, Paul, John, Susan   ☐

Can repeat

I have a red car.   ☐

The dog is running to the house.   ☐

I can see the bird in the tall tree.   ☐

I went to the store to buy candy, and apples, and oranges.   ☐

Auditory Discrimination

Identifies common sounds in environment   ☐

Can identify words ending in given sound   ☐

Can identify words beginning with given sound   ☐

Can identify rhyming words   ☐

Can supply 3 words ending in *ing*   ☐

Can supply 3 words beginning with *ca*   ☐

                                  m   ☐

                                  si   ☐

Listing of Catalog Companies

Code	Company Name and Address
ABC	ABC School Supply 6500 Peachtree Industrial Blvd./P.O. Box 4750 Norcross, Georgia 30091
CC	C. C. Publications, Inc. P.O. Box 23699 Tigard, Oregon 97233-0108
Child	Childcraft Education Corporation 20 Kilmer Road/P.O. Box 3081 Edison, New Jersey 08818-3081
CS	Communication Skill Builders, Inc. 3130 N. Dodge Blvd./P.O. Box 42050 Tucson, Arizona 85733
CP	Constructive Playthings 1227 E. 119th Street Grandview, Missouri 64030
DX	DIDAX Educational Resources 6 Doulton Place Peabody, Massachusetts 01960
DLM	DLM Teaching Resources One DLM Park/P.O. Box 4000 Allen, Texas 75002
ETA	E. T. A. 199 Carpenter Ave. Wheeling, Illinois 60090
Lake	Lakeshore Curriculum Materials Company 2695 E. Dominguez St./P.O. Box 6261 Carson, California 90749

Build your students' strengths with these materials . . .

TOTAL: Teacher Organized Training for Acquisition of Language (1983)
by Beth Witt and Jeanne Boose
Here's a comprehensive language curriculum with lessons and activities for every day of the school year. TOTAL contains 15 teaching units that train and reinforce a 250-word vocabulary (both verbally and in sign language). This basic, functional core vocabulary is stressed again and again through— games, songs, art activities, 175 teaching pictures and full-color photographs, coloring pictures and worksheets, and 15 storybooks. Help your preschool and language-delayed children learn the communication skills they need.
Catalog No. 4619-Y $299

ALL ABOUT ME: Activities for Learning Language (1986)
by Constance F. McCarthy and Ann D. Sheehy
Help younger children develop pragmatic language skills and improve self-image with this new collection of reproducible activities. These worksheets provide children with opportunities to learn and use basic language skills in developing self-awareness. You'll have worksheets for these topics—colors, shapes, concepts, senses, feelings, self-expression, body parts, clothing, and sequencing.   **Catalog No. 7290-Y $13.95**

**ART, FINE MOTOR, AND COGNITIVE IDEAS FOR SPECIAL
EDUCATION** (1986)   *by Susan J. Smith, Ed.D.*
These practical activities and strategies can help you individualize your instruction. This handy book is full of ideas for classroom organization, independent projects, and pre-vocational training. Activities are designed to increase the student's ability to stay on task, develop fine motor skills and creative talents, and offer ways to use leisure time.
Catalog No. 7281-Y $8.95

NATURAL LANGUAGE (Revised 1981)
by John Hatten, Ph.D., and Pequetti Hatten
Parents will use this book because it's easy to understand. Here's how to involve parents in the language teaching process with activities that are easy, fun, and effective. These activities work because they are enjoyable, natural, and encourage active parent participation.   **Catalog No. 2026-Y $7.95**

EMERGING LANGUAGE 3 (Revised 1981)
by John Hatten, Ph.D., Tracy Goman, and Carol Lent
These 164 activities offer experiences and procedures for specific language goals. With this handbook you'll have a practical, sequenced program for maximizing a child's responses and involvement in language training. It follows "normal" language development from single-word utterances to basic sentence modification.   **Catalog No. 2028-Y $7.95**

Communication ®
Skill Builders
3130 N. Dodge Blvd./P.O. Box 42050
Tucson, Arizona 85733
.(602) 323-7500